The Evolution of Communication and Information Technologies

Calvin R. Johnson

The Evolution of Communication and Information Technologies

Title: The Evolution of Communication and Information Technologies

Library of Congress Card Catalog Number: 2023914356

ISBN: 9798854327121

Published by: C R Johnson Group

Cover Design: Leyeama Johnson

Editors: Leyeama Johnson, Lainu Johnson

Credits: The author would like to extend gratitude to all contributors, researchers, and industry experts whose work and insights have enriched this book.

For permissions and inquiries, please contact the publisher at:

C R Johnson Group Email: calvin.johnson@comcast.net

Printed in the United States of America

First Printing: [2023]

This book is dedicated to the pursuit of knowledge and the advancement of Communication and Information Technologies. May it inspire readers to innovate, collaborate, and create sustainable and customer-centric Information Technologies that shape a better tomorrow and benefit mankind.

The Evolution of Communication and Information Technologies

Table of Contents: **Page**

Chapter 1   **8**

Introduction

- o Purpose of the Book
- o Definition of Communication and Information Technologies
- o Importance of Studying the Evolution of Communication and Information Technologies

Chapter 2   **12**

The Early Origins of Communication

- o Prehistoric Communication Techniques
- o Ancient Writing Systems
- o Development of Postal Services

Chapter 3   **16**

The Printing Press and the Spread of Information

- o Gutenberg's Invention
- o Impact on Knowledge Dissemination
- o Printing Press Innovations

The Evolution of Communication and Information Technologies

Chapter 4   *20*

Telegraph and the Birth of Long-Distance communication

- o   Samuel Morse and the Telegraph

- o   The Role of Telegraph in Industrialization and Globalization

- o   Advancements in Telegraph Technology

Chapter 5   *23*

The Telephone and the Rise of Voice Communication

- o   Alexander Graham Bell and the Invention of the Telephone

- o   Telephone Networks and Infrastructure

- o   Mobile Telephony and Wireless Communication

Chapter 6   *25*

Radio and Broadcast Communication

- o   Guglielmo Marconi and Radio Transmission

- o   Early Radio Broadcasting

- o   Commercialization of Radio and Emergence of Public Broadcasting

Chapter 7   *28*

Television and the Visual Era

- o   Early Experiments in Television

The Evolution of Communication and Information Technologies

- o   The Rise of Television as a Mass Medium

- o   Technological Advancements in Television Broadcasting

Chapter 8   *31*

The Internet and the Digital Revolution

- o   Birth of the Internet

- o   World Wide Web and Hypertext

- o   Emergence of E-commerce and Online Services

Chapter 9   *35*

Mobile Devices and the Era of Ubiquitous Communication

- o   Development of Mobile Phones

- o   Smartphone Revolution

- o   Mobile Applications and Connectivity

Chapter 10   *38*

Social Media and the Age of Online Interaction

- o   Evolution of Social Media Platforms

- o   Impact of Social Media on Communication and Society

- o   Privacy and Ethical Considerations

Chapter 11   *42*

The Internet of Things (IoT) and Connected Devices

The Evolution of Communication and Information Technologies

- o   Definition and Scope of IoT

- o   Applications of IoT in Various Sectors

- o   Challenges and Future Prospects of IoT

Chapter 12   **45**

Artificial Intelligence and Communication Technologies

- o   Introduction to Artificial Intelligence

- o   AI Applications in Communication

- o   Ethical Implications of AI in Communication

Chapter 13   **48**

Virtual and Augmented Reality in Communication

- o   Virtual Reality (VR) and Augmented Reality (AR) Explained

- o   Applications of VR and AR in Communication

- o   Future Possibilities and Impact

Chapter 14   **52**

Future Trends and Technologies in Communication

- o   5G and Beyond

- o   Quantum Communication

- o   Brain-Computer Interfaces

Conclusion   **55**

The Evolution of Communication and Information Technologies

- o Recap of the Evolution of Communication and Information Technologies

- o Reflection on the Impact of Communication Technologies on Society

- o Future Prospects and Possibilities

References   ***58***

Selected Sources for Further Reading   **61**

Appendices: ***64***

- Glossary of Terms

- Timeline of Key Communication and Information Technology Milestones

- Profiles of Notable Inventors and Innovators

- Selected Further Reading

- About the Author

Note: This table of contents provides an overview of the book's structure and topics. The actual content of the book will delve into each subject in detail, examining historical context, technological advancements, social impact, and future implications.

The Evolution of Communication and Information Technologies

Chapter 1: Introduction

In this chapter, we will embark on a journey to explore the fascinating evolution of communication and information technologies. We will begin by understanding the purpose of this book, defining the concepts of communication and information technologies, and delving into the significance of studying their evolution. By laying this foundation, we can better appreciate the profound impact these technologies have had on society.

1.1 Purpose of the Book

The purpose of this book is to provide a comprehensive exploration of the evolution of communication and information technologies throughout history. We will delve into the origins of communication methods, the development of groundbreaking inventions, and the transformative effects of these technologies on various aspects of human life.

By examining the historical progression, technological advancements, and societal implications, we aim to offer readers a deeper understanding of how communication and information technologies have shaped and continue to shape our world. Through this exploration, we can gain insights into the present state of these technologies and glimpse into the future possibilities they hold.

The Evolution of Communication and Information Technologies

1.2 Definition of Communication and Information Technologies

Communication can be defined as the process of exchanging information, ideas, thoughts, and emotions between individuals, groups, or mass audiences. It encompasses verbal and non-verbal forms of expression, including speech, writing, gestures, and visual cues. Communication serves as the bedrock of human interaction, allowing us to convey and receive messages, establish connections, and share knowledge.

Information technologies, on the other hand, refer to the tools, systems, and processes used to create, store, transmit, and manage information. These technologies encompass a wide range of devices, networks, and software applications that facilitate the flow of information across various channels and mediums.

In the context of this book, communication and information technologies are intimately connected. Communication technologies provide the means to transmit information, enabling individuals and societies to communicate over vast distances and across barriers of time and space. Information technologies, in turn, empower the storage, processing, and dissemination of information, enhancing the efficiency and accessibility of communication.

1.3 Importance of Studying the Evolution of Communication and Information Technologies

Studying the evolution of communication and information technologies is crucial for several reasons:

1.3.1 Historical Significance: The evolution of communication and information technologies is intertwined with the course of human history.

The Evolution of Communication and Information Technologies

Understanding how communication methods and tools have evolved over time allows us to appreciate the progress made and the challenges faced by previous generations. It provides valuable insights into the societal, cultural, and economic shifts that have shaped our world.

1.3.2 Technological Advancements: By examining the evolution of these technologies, we can trace the key inventions and innovations that have propelled society forward. From ancient writing systems to the Internet and beyond, each advancement has built upon the foundations laid by its predecessors. Studying these advancements helps us comprehend the intricate web of technological progress and the potential for future breakthroughs.

1.3.3 Social Impact: Communication and information technologies have had a profound impact on various aspects of human life, including education, commerce, governance, and entertainment. They have altered the way we interact, work, and access information. By studying their evolution, we can gain a deeper understanding of the societal transformations brought about by these technologies and explore their implications for the future.

1.3.4 Future Implications: The study of the evolution of communication and information technologies enables us to anticipate future trends and possibilities. By examining the trajectory of technological advancements, we can envision potential scenarios and prepare for the challenges and opportunities that lie ahead. It empowers us to make informed decisions and shape the direction of these technologies in a way that aligns with our values and aspirations.

The Evolution of Communication and Information Technologies

In the subsequent chapters of this book, we will embark on an enlightening journey through time, exploring the key milestones, inventions, and societal changes that have shaped the evolution of communication and information technologies. By the end of this book, it is our hope that readers will gain a comprehensive understanding of this fascinating subject and develop a deeper appreciation for the transformative power of these technologies.

Thank you for joining us on this exploration of the evolution of communication and information technologies. Let us now embark on this enlightening journey through history and innovation.

Chapter 2: The Early Origins of Communication

2.1 Prehistoric Communication Techniques

Before the development of written language, early humans relied on various forms of communication to convey information and express ideas. These prehistoric communication techniques laid the groundwork for the evolution of human interaction and paved the way for future advancements. Some notable prehistoric communication methods include:

2.1.1 Oral Tradition: Oral tradition, also known as oral history, refers to the transmission of knowledge, stories, and cultural practices through spoken word. This form of communication played a crucial role in early societies, allowing information to be passed down from one generation to the next. Through oral traditions, early humans preserved their histories, myths, and cultural values, fostering a sense of community and identity.

2.1.2 Cave Paintings and Petroglyphs: Prehistoric cave paintings and petroglyphs, found in various regions of the world, provide a window into early human communication. These visual representations depicted scenes from daily life, animals, hunting techniques, and spiritual beliefs. They served as a means of communication, possibly conveying messages related to rituals, storytelling, and communal identity.

2.1.3 Smoke Signals and Drumbeats: In areas where long-distance communication was necessary, early civilizations developed methods such as smoke signals and drumbeats. Smoke signals involved creating distinctive patterns of smoke to convey messages across vast distances. Drumbeats, on the other hand, allowed for rhythmic patterns to be used as a form of communication, carrying messages over significant distances in a way that could be understood by trained listeners.

2.2 Ancient Writing Systems

The advent of writing systems marked a significant milestone in human communication, enabling the preservation and dissemination of information beyond the limitations of oral tradition. Ancient civilizations developed various writing systems that revolutionized communication and laid the foundation for future advancements in literacy and knowledge transfer. Some noteworthy ancient writing systems include:

2.2.1 Sumerian Cuneiform: The Sumerians of Mesopotamia (modern-day Iraq) are credited with developing one of the earliest known writing systems, called cuneiform. This system involved pressing wedge-shaped marks on clay tablets using a stylus. It initially served administrative purposes but eventually expanded to encompass literature, laws, religious texts, and historical records.

2.2.2 Egyptian Hieroglyphs: The ancient Egyptians developed a complex writing system known as hieroglyphs. Hieroglyphs were pictorial symbols that represented objects, ideas, and sounds. The script was used for religious texts, royal decrees, and monumental inscriptions. The decipherment of hieroglyphs in the early 19th century opened a wealth of knowledge about ancient Egyptian civilization.

2.2.3 Chinese Script: The Chinese script, dating back to the Shang Dynasty (c. 1600–1046 BCE), is one of the oldest surviving writing systems. Chinese characters, representing both sound and meaning, are used in written Chinese, Japanese, and Korean languages. The complexity of the script contributed to the preservation of Chinese culture and history over thousands of years.

2.3 Development of Postal Services

As civilizations expanded and trade networks grew, the need for efficient long-distance communication became evident. Postal services emerged as organized systems for the transportation and delivery of messages, connecting people across vast distances. Some key developments in the evolution of postal services include:

2.3.1 Ancient Messengers: In ancient times, the delivery of messages relied on human messengers who traveled on foot, horseback, or by boat. These messengers carried important communications, diplomatic dispatches, and news between cities and empires. The Persian Empire, for example, established a sophisticated courier system known as the Royal Road, facilitating communication across its vast territories.

2.3.2 Ancient Postal Networks: The Roman Empire created an extensive postal network called the *cursus publicus*, which allowed for the rapid transmission of messages, military dispatches, and official communications. The system featured waystations and relay stations where messengers could rest and exchange horses, enabling faster delivery over long distances.

2.3.3 Development of Postal Systems in China: China developed a postal system as early as the Han Dynasty (202 BCE–220 CE). This system, known as the Great Wall Postal Service, utilized horses and trained couriers to transport official correspondence and documents. The Tang Dynasty (618–

The Evolution of Communication and Information Technologies

907 CE) further expanded and formalized the postal service, establishing a network of relay stations, postal routes, and standardized postal rates.

The early origins of communication laid the groundwork for the development of more advanced communication and information technologies. From prehistoric oral traditions to the emergence of ancient writing systems and the establishment of postal networks, these early methods of communication provided the foundation for the rich tapestry of human interaction that continues to evolve to this day. In the following chapters, we will delve further into the remarkable advancements in communication and information technologies throughout history.

The Evolution of Communication and Information Technologies

Chapter 3: The Printing Press and the Spread of Information

The printing press, one of the most revolutionary inventions in human history, transformed the way information was disseminated and had a profound impact on society. In this chapter, we will explore the invention of the printing press by Johannes Gutenberg, its transformative effect on knowledge dissemination, and the subsequent innovations that further enhanced its capabilities.

3.1 Gutenberg's Invention

Johannes Gutenberg, a German goldsmith, and inventor is credited with the invention of the printing press in the mid-15th century. Gutenberg's invention combined several existing technologies, including movable type, oil-based ink, and the wine press, to create a highly efficient and scalable printing system.

The key innovation of Gutenberg's printing press was the introduction of movable type. Instead of carving an entire page of text on a wooden block, Gutenberg created individual metal letters that could be rearranged and reused. This allowed for faster typesetting and increased the speed of printing significantly. Gutenberg's printing press also employed oil-based ink, which adhered well to paper and produced clearer, and more durable prints compared to the water-based inks used previously.

In 1455, Gutenberg printed his most famous work, the Gutenberg Bible, a complete Latin translation of the Bible. This monumental achievement demonstrated the power and potential of the printing press, marking the beginning of a new era in the dissemination of knowledge.

The Evolution of Communication and Information Technologies

3.2 Impact on Knowledge Dissemination

The invention of the printing press had a profound impact on knowledge dissemination, leading to a series of transformative changes in society:

3.2.1 Mass Production of Books: Before the printing press, books were laboriously copied by hand, making them expensive and scarce. Gutenberg's invention revolutionized the production of books by enabling mass production. Books became more affordable and accessible to a larger segment of the population, democratizing access to knowledge and information.

3.2.2 Preservation and Standardization of Knowledge: With the ability to produce multiple copies of texts, the printing press facilitated the preservation and standardization of knowledge. Ideas, discoveries, and cultural works could be reproduced with greater accuracy, ensuring their longevity and widespread availability. This standardization of knowledge fostered the growth of intellectual discourse and the advancement of various fields, including science, philosophy, and literature.

3.2.3 Expansion of Literacy: The printing press played a crucial role in expanding literacy rates. As books became more affordable and readily available, the demand for literacy increased. The dissemination of printed materials, including newspapers, pamphlets, and educational texts, facilitated the spread of literacy among the general population. Literacy, in turn, empowered individuals to engage in critical thinking, participate in public discourse, and contribute to social progress.

3.2.4 Cultural and Religious Reformation: The printing press played a significant role in the cultural and religious reformation movements of the

16th century. It enabled the rapid dissemination of Martin Luther's Ninety- Five Theses, sparking the Protestant Reformation. The printing press allowed religious texts and reformist ideas to spread quickly, challenging the authority of the Catholic Church and contributing to the diversification of religious thought.

3.3 Printing Press Innovations

Following Gutenberg's initial invention, subsequent innovators made further advancements to the printing press, enhancing its capabilities, and expanding its applications:

3.3.1 Improvements in Press Design: Innovators such as William Caxton and Richard M. Hoe made significant improvements to the design of the printing press. These advancements included the introduction of iron hand presses and steam-powered rotary presses, which increased the speed and efficiency of printing.

3.3.2 Typeface Development: Typeface design evolved over time, with notable contributions from printers like Claude Garamond, William Caslon, and John Baskerville. They developed distinct typefaces, refining legibility, elegance, and readability. Typeface design became an art form and contributed to the aesthetic appeal of printed materials.

3.3.3 Industrial Printing and Newspaper Production: In the 19th century, the industrial revolution propelled further advancements in printing technology. Steam-powered presses, high-speed rotary presses, and the introduction of continuous paper rolls allowed for the rapid production of newspapers, magazines, and other printed materials on a large scale. This

The Evolution of Communication and Information Technologies

facilitated the rise of mass media and the spread of information to a wider audience.

The printing press revolutionized the way information was disseminated, fueling the spread of knowledge, the exchange of ideas, and the progress of society. Gutenberg's invention paved the way for a new era of information sharing, contributing to cultural, intellectual, and societal transformations. In the subsequent chapters, we will continue our exploration of the evolution of communication and information technologies, uncovering further breakthroughs and their impact on human communication.

The Evolution of Communication and Information Technologies

Chapter 4: Telegraph and the Birth of Long-Distance Communication

4.1 Samuel Morse and the Telegraph

The invention of the telegraph revolutionized long-distance communication, allowing messages to be transmitted quickly across vast distances. One of the key figures in the development of the telegraph was Samuel Morse, an American inventor and artist. In 1837, Morse, along with his assistant Alfred Vail, successfully demonstrated the first practical telegraph system.

Morse's telegraph used electrical signals to transmit coded messages over long distances. The system employed a telegraph key to tap out a series of dots and dashes, known as Morse code, which represented letters and numbers. These electrical signals traveled along a wire, allowing messages to be sent and received almost instantaneously.

4.2 The Role of Telegraph in Industrialization and Globalization

The telegraph played a crucial role in driving industrialization and globalization during the 19th century. Its impact can be seen in several key areas:

4.2.1 Rapid Communication: The telegraph enabled near-instantaneous communication across great distances, revolutionizing the speed at which information could be transmitted. This was particularly significant for business and commerce, as it facilitated faster transactions, coordination of operations, and exchange of market information. The telegraph also transformed news reporting, enabling the rapid dissemination of information across regions and connecting people like never before.

4.2.2 Transportation and Logistics: The telegraph revolutionized transportation and logistics by facilitating real-time communication between distant locations. It allowed for the coordination of train schedules, track maintenance, and the movement of goods, leading to more efficient and reliable transportation networks. This, in turn, fueled the growth of industries such as railroads, shipping, and trade.

4.2.3 Global Connectivity: The telegraph facilitated global connectivity by linking different regions and continents. Transoceanic telegraph cables were laid, connecting continents such as Europe, North America, and Asia. This allowed for instantaneous communication across vast distances and contributed to the emergence of a global network of information exchange and commerce.

4.3 Advancements in Telegraph Technology

Over time, advancements in telegraph technology further improved its efficiency, reach, and capabilities. Some notable advancements include:

4.3.1 Submarine Telegraph Cables: The development of submarine telegraph cables allowed for direct communication between continents across oceans. The first successful transatlantic cable was laid in 1858, connecting North America and Europe. Subsequent advancements in cable design and insulation materials improved the reliability and speed of transoceanic telegraph communication.

4.3.2 Automatic Telegraph Systems: In the late 19th and early 20th centuries, automatic telegraph systems were introduced. These systems used punched paper tape to encode and transmit messages automatically, eliminating the need for manual Morse code operators. Automatic telegraph systems significantly increased the speed and efficiency of telegraph communication.

4.3.3 Multiplexing and Printing Telegraphs: Multiplexing technology allowed for multiple messages to be transmitted simultaneously over a single telegraph line, improving efficiency and capacity. Additionally, printing telegraphs, such as the famous "Stock Ticker," automatically print incoming messages, making them more accessible and easier to read.

The Evolution of Communication and Information Technologies

Chapter 5: The Telephone and the Rise of Voice Communication

5.1 Alexander Graham Bell and the Invention of the Telephone

The invention of the telephone marked a significant milestone in communication technology, as it introduced the transmission of voice over long distances. Alexander Graham Bell, a Scottish-born inventor, is credited with inventing the telephone in 1876.

Bell's telephone used electric currents to transmit sound vibrations, allowing for the reproduction of human speech. It consisted of a transmitter, which converted sound waves into electrical signals, and a receiver, which converted the electrical signals back into audible sound. The telephone revolutionized communication by enabling individuals to have real-time voice conversations across great distances.

5.2 Telephone Networks and Infrastructure

The widespread adoption of telephones necessitated the development of telephone networks and infrastructure. Telephone exchanges, consisting of switchboards and operators, were established to connect callers and facilitate the routing of calls. Initially, these exchanges were manually operated, with operators physically plugging and unplugging cables to establish connections. However, advancements in switching technology eventually led to the automation of telephone exchanges.

As telephone networks expanded, infrastructure such as telephone poles, cables, and later underground lines, were laid to provide connectivity between locations. These networks connected towns, cities, and eventually entire countries, enabling individuals to communicate over long distances with ease.

The Evolution of Communication and Information Technologies

5.3 Mobile Telephony and Wireless Communication

The advent of mobile telephony and wireless communication further revolutionized the way people communicate. Mobile phones allowed individuals to make and receive calls while on the move, providing unprecedented convenience and accessibility. The development of cellular networks enabled seamless communication over larger geographical areas by dividing regions into smaller cells, each served by a base station.

Advancements in wireless communication technologies, such as 3G, 4G, and now 5G, have further enhanced mobile telephony by providing faster data transmission, improved call quality, and support for multimedia applications. These advancements have transformed mobile phones into multifunctional devices capable of internet browsing, messaging, video calling, and much more.

The invention of the telephone and the subsequent development of mobile telephony and wireless communication have greatly impacted human interaction and connectivity. These technologies have connected people across vast distances, facilitating real-time voice communication and contributing to the globalization of society.

In the following chapters, we will continue to explore the evolution of communication and information technologies, uncovering more remarkable advancements and their societal impact.

The Evolution of Communication and Information Technologies

Chapter 6: Radio and Broadcast Communication

6.1 Guglielmo Marconi and Radio Transmission

The invention of radio transmission revolutionized communication by allowing wireless transmission of signals across long distances. Guglielmo Marconi, an Italian inventor, and electrical engineer is widely credited with the development of practical radio technology in the late 19th and early 20th centuries.

Marconi's experiments with radio transmission led to the invention of the wireless telegraph, which used electromagnetic waves to carry signals without the need for physical wires. In 1901, he achieved a significant milestone by successfully transmitting the first transatlantic radio signal, demonstrating the immense potential of wireless communication.

6.2 Early Radio Broadcasting

Following Marconi's groundbreaking work, radio broadcasting emerged as a means of transmitting audio content to a wide audience. In the early 20th century, pioneering individuals and organizations began experimenting with radio broadcasting techniques:

6.2.1 Reginald Fessenden: Reginald Fessenden, a Canadian inventor, made significant contributions to early radio broadcasting. In 1906, he successfully transmitted voice and music over radio waves, becoming the first person to broadcast audio content. Fessenden's experimental broadcasts laid the foundation for the future development of radio as a medium for entertainment and information dissemination.

6.2.2 Radio Amateurs: Amateur radio operators, or "hams," played a crucial role in the early days of radio broadcasting. These enthusiasts experimented with radio technology, establishing connections, and exchanging messages over the airwaves. They contributed to the growth of radio as a hobby and played a part in the development of broadcasting techniques and equipment.

6.3 Commercialization of Radio and Emergence of Public Broadcasting

As radio technology advanced, the commercialization of radio broadcasting began to take shape. The following developments marked significant milestones in the expansion and diversification of radio as a medium:

6.3.1 Commercial Radio Stations: In the 1920s, the establishment of commercial radio stations laid the foundation for the broadcasting industry. These stations operated by private entities and aimed to generate revenue through advertising and sponsorship. They offered a variety of programs, including news, music, dramas, and comedy shows, catering to diverse audience interests.

6.3.2 Emergence of Public Broadcasting: Alongside commercial radio, the concept of public broadcasting also emerged. Public broadcasting aimed to serve the public interest by providing educational, cultural, and informative content. Publicly funded radio stations, such as the British Broadcasting Corporation (BBC) and the Australian Broadcasting Corporation (ABC), were established to offer programming that was independent of commercial interests and accessible to all citizens.

6.3.3 Radio Networks and Syndication: Radio networks began to emerge, connecting multiple stations and enabling the distribution of programming

The Evolution of Communication and Information Technologies

across a wider area. Networks such as the National Broadcasting Company (NBC) and the Columbia Broadcasting System (CBS) in the United States played a significant role in the growth and standardization of radio broadcasting. Syndication of popular programs allowed for the sharing of content among multiple stations, expanding the reach and popularity of certain shows.

The commercialization of radio broadcasting and the emergence of public broadcasting transformed the way people accessed and consumed audio content. Radio became a powerful medium for entertainment, news dissemination, and cultural expression, bringing a shared experience to diverse audiences.

In the subsequent chapters, we will continue to explore the evolution of communication and information technologies, uncovering more remarkable advancements and their impact on human communication and society.

Chapter 7: Television and the Visual Era

7.1 Early Experiments in Television

The development of television marked a groundbreaking leap in communication technology, enabling the transmission of moving images and sound over long distances. Early pioneers conducted experiments that laid the foundation for television as we know it today:

7.1.1 Paul Nipkow and the Nipkow Disk: In the late 19th century, Paul Nipkow, a German engineer, invented the Nipkow disk, a mechanical device that could scan images line by line. This invention formed the basis of the first electromechanical television systems. The Nipkow disk enabled the conversion of visual information into electrical signals, which could be transmitted and reconstructed as images.

7.1.2 Vladimir Zworykin and the Iconoscope: Russian-born engineer Vladimir Zworykin made significant contributions to the development of television. He invented the iconoscope, an electronic camera tube that could capture and convert light into electrical signals. The iconoscope revolutionized television technology by enabling the electronic scanning and transmission of images.

7.2 The Rise of Television as a Mass Medium

Television quickly emerged as a dominant mass medium, captivating audiences with its ability to deliver audiovisual content directly to their homes. Several key factors contributed to its rapid rise:

7.2.1 Public Broadcasting: Public broadcasting played a vital role in the early days of television. Publicly funded networks, such as the British

The Evolution of Communication and Information Technologies

Broadcasting Corporation (BBC) and the National Broadcasting Company (NBC) in the United States, provided educational, cultural, and news programs to the public. Public broadcasting helped ensure a diverse range of programming and laid the foundation for television's role as a source of information and entertainment.

7.2.2 Popularization of Television Sets: As television technology matured, the cost of television sets decreased, making them more affordable for the public. The availability of television sets in households grew rapidly, expanding the reach and influence of television as a medium.

7.2.3 Impact on Popular Culture: Television became a central aspect of popular culture, influencing entertainment, fashion, advertising, and social dynamics. It provided a shared experience for families and communities, with popular shows and events becoming cultural touchstones. Television shaped public opinion, introduced new ideas, and brought the world into people's living rooms.

7.3 Technological Advancements in Television Broadcasting

Technological advancements further enhanced the capabilities and appeal of television broadcasting:

7.3.1 Introduction of Color Television: The transition from black and white to color television was a significant milestone. Color television sets and compatible broadcasting systems were introduced, enriching the visual experience, and bringing vibrant images to viewers' screens. The adoption of color broadcasting gradually became widespread, enhancing the realism and visual impact of televised content.

The Evolution of Communication and Information Technologies

7.3.2 Advancements in Broadcast Standards: Broadcast standards evolved over time, leading to improvements in picture quality, sound clarity, and signal transmission. Innovations such as high-definition television (HDTV), digital television (DTV), and advanced audio systems provided viewers with enhanced audiovisual experiences.

7.3.3 Cable and Satellite Television: The introduction of cable and satellite television expanded the range of available channels and improved signal quality. Cable networks offered specialized programming and premium channels, while satellite television enabled global broadcasting and increased access to international content.

The advent of television transformed the way people consumed information and entertainment. The visual medium of television brought the world into people's homes, shaping cultures, fostering shared experiences, and influencing societal dynamics.

In the subsequent chapters, we will continue our exploration of the evolution of communication and information technologies, uncovering more remarkable advancements and their impact on human communication and society.

The Evolution of Communication and Information Technologies

Chapter 8: The Internet and the Digital Revolution

8.1 Birth of the Internet

The Internet stands as one of the most transformative inventions in the history of communication and information technologies. It emerged as a global network of interconnected computer systems, revolutionizing the way people access information, communicate, and conduct various activities. The development of the Internet can be traced back to several key milestones:

8.1.1 ARPANET: The Advanced Research Projects Agency Network (ARPANET), created by the United States Department of Defense in the late 1960s, laid the foundation for the Internet. ARPANET was designed as a decentralized network that allowed multiple computers to communicate and share resources. It served as a precursor to the modern Internet.

8.1.2 TCP/IP: The Transmission Control Protocol/Internet Protocol (TCP/IP) emerged as the standard protocol suite for data transmission over the Internet. Developed in the 1970s, TCP/IP provided the framework for data packets to be routed across multiple networks, ensuring reliable and efficient communication between computers.

8.1.3 Commercialization and Global Expansion: In the late 1980s and early 1990s, the Internet transitioned from a predominantly academic and military network to a commercial and global phenomenon. The deregulation of the telecommunications industry and advancements in networking technologies paved the way for widespread Internet access and usage.

8.2 World Wide Web and Hypertext

The World Wide Web (WWW), developed by Sir Tim Berners-Lee in the late 1980s, revolutionized the way information was organized, accessed, and shared on the Internet. The WWW introduced the concept of hypertext, which allowed users to navigate between interconnected documents using hyperlinks. Key aspects of the World Wide Web include:

8.2.1 Hyperlinks and Web Pages: Hyperlinks enabled users to navigate between web pages by clicking on text, images, or other elements. Web pages, written in Hypertext Markup Language (HTML), could include various types of content such as text, images, videos, and interactive elements.

8.2.2 Web Browsers: Web browsers, such as Mosaic, Netscape Navigator, and later Internet Explorer and Mozilla Firefox, provided user-friendly interfaces for accessing and interacting with web pages. Browsers allowed users to view web content, follow hyperlinks, and interact with online services.

8.2.3 Search Engines: Search engines, such as Google and Yahoo!, played a pivotal role in facilitating information discovery on the web. These tools allowed users to search for specific content by entering keywords, enabling efficient access to a vast amount of information available on the Internet.

8.3 Emergence of E-commerce and Online Services

The Internet brought about a digital revolution, transforming commerce, and introducing a wide range of online services. The following developments shaped the emergence of e-commerce and online services:

The Evolution of Communication and Information Technologies

8.3.1 E-commerce: The Internet provided a platform for conducting commercial transactions electronically. Online marketplaces, such as Amazon and eBay, enabled individuals and businesses to buy and sell products and services globally. Secure online payment systems, including PayPal and credit card processors, facilitated safe and convenient financial transactions.

8.3.2 Online Services: The Internet revolutionized service industries, offering a multitude of online services. Social media platforms, such as Facebook and Twitter, transformed communication and social interactions. Streaming services, such as Netflix and Spotify, allowed users to access on-demand entertainment. Online banking, travel booking, and education platforms, among others, expanded the accessibility and convenience of various services.

8.3.3 Information Accessibility and Sharing: The Internet democratized access to information, enabling users to search for and access a vast array of knowledge. Online encyclopedias, digital libraries, and open-access resources provided unprecedented opportunities for learning and research. The rise of user-generated content platforms, such as Wikipedia and blogging platforms, facilitated information sharing and collaboration on a global scale.

The Internet and the digital revolution have transformed the way people communicate, access information, and conduct business. The World Wide Web introduced a new paradigm of interconnectedness, while the emergence of e-commerce and online services opened up new avenues for commerce and digital experiences.

The Evolution of Communication and Information Technologies

In the subsequent chapters, we will continue our exploration of the evolution of communication and information technologies, uncovering more remarkable advancements and their impact on human communication and society.

The Evolution of Communication and Information Technologies

Chapter 9: Mobile Devices and the Era of Ubiquitous Communication

9.1 Development of Mobile Phones

The development of mobile phones revolutionized communication by providing individuals with the ability to connect and communicate while on the move. The evolution of mobile phones can be traced through several key milestones:

9.1.1 Early Mobile Telephony: The first mobile telephone systems were introduced in the mid-20th century. These systems used analog technology and required large, cumbersome devices. Mobile phones were primarily used by professionals and individuals with specific needs, such as emergency services personnel.

9.1.2 Introduction of Cellular Networks: In the 1980s, cellular networks were introduced, allowing for greater coverage and capacity in mobile communication. Cellular technology divided regions into cells, each served by a base station, providing improved signal quality and call reliability.

9.1.3 Advancements in Mobile Technologies: Advancements in mobile technology led to the development of smaller, more portable phones. Digital cellular networks, such as GSM (Global System for Mobile Communications), offered enhanced voice quality and the ability to send short text messages (SMS).

9.2 Smartphone Revolution

The introduction of smartphones marked a transformative shift in mobile communication. Smartphones combined the functionalities of a mobile

The Evolution of Communication and Information Technologies

phone with advanced computing capabilities, revolutionizing the way people access information and interact with technology:

9.2.1 Rise of the iPhone and Android: The launch of the iPhone by Apple in 2007 and the subsequent introduction of the Android operating system by Google in 2008 sparked the smartphone revolution. These devices featured touchscreens, intuitive user interfaces, and access to mobile applications, setting the stage for the proliferation of smartphones.

9.2.2 App Stores and Mobile Applications: App stores, such as Apple's App Store and Google Play Store, enabled users to browse and download a wide range of mobile applications. Mobile apps transformed smartphones into versatile tools for communication, productivity, entertainment, and countless other functions.

9.2.3 Integration of Internet Connectivity: Smartphones seamlessly integrate internet connectivity, enabling users to access websites, browse the web, and use online services from anywhere with a mobile data or Wi- Fi connection. This facilitated real-time communication, information retrieval, and access to cloud-based services.

9.3 Mobile Applications and Connectivity

Mobile applications, or apps, became a defining feature of smartphones, driving innovation and transforming various industries:

9.3.1 Communication and Social Media Apps: Messaging apps, such as WhatsApp and WeChat, allow users to exchange text, voice, and multimedia messages instantly. Social media platforms, including Facebook, Instagram, and Twitter, enabled users to connect, share updates, and engage in social interactions on a global scale.

The Evolution of Communication and Information Technologies

9.3.2 Productivity and Utility Apps: Mobile apps revolutionized productivity, offering tools for email management, document editing, note - taking, task organization, and more. Utility apps provided functionalities such as navigation, weather updates, translation, and financial management, enhancing convenience and accessibility.

9.3.3 Entertainment and Media Apps: Mobile devices became popular platforms for entertainment consumption. Streaming apps, such as Netflix and Spotify, allowed users to access movies, TV shows, music, and podcasts on the go. Mobile gaming also experienced significant growth, with millions of users enjoying a wide range of games on their smartphones.

9.3.4 E-commerce and Mobile Payments: Mobile devices facilitated the growth of e-commerce through dedicated shopping apps, enabling users to browse, shop, and make secure online purchases. Mobile payment systems, including digital wallets and contactless payment methods, simplified transactions and transformed retail experiences.

The ubiquity of mobile devices and the proliferation of mobile applications have made communication and access to information pervasive in everyday life. Smartphones have become an integral part of modern society, transforming the way people communicate, work, entertain themselves, and navigate the world.

In the subsequent chapters, we will continue our exploration of the evolution of communication and information technologies, uncovering more remarkable advancements and their impact on human communication and society.

The Evolution of Communication and Information Technologies

Chapter 10: Social Media and the Age of Online Interaction

10.1 Evolution of Social Media Platforms

Social media platforms have transformed the way people interact, communicate, and share information online. The evolution of social media can be traced through several key stages:

10.1.1 Early Online Communities: In the late 20th century, online communities emerged, providing platforms for people with common interests to connect and share information. Platforms like Usenet, IRC (Internet Relay Chat), and early web-based forums laid the foundation for the social interactions that would later define social media.

10.1.2 Emergence of Social Networking Sites: The early 2000s saw the rise of social networking sites, such as Friendster, MySpace, and later Facebook. These platforms allowed users to create profiles, connect with friends, and share content. They introduced the concept of a "social graph," representing the connections between individuals within a network.

10.1.3 Microblogging and Real-Time Updates: Microblogging platforms like Twitter emerged, enabling users to share short updates and engage in real-time conversations. Twitter's 140-character limit encouraged concise and immediate communication, leading to the popularization of hashtags and viral trends.

10.1.4 Visual Sharing and Multimedia Platforms: Platforms like Instagram and Snapchat brought visual content to the forefront, allowing users to share photos and videos with filters, effects, and storytelling features. These platforms emphasized visual communication, creativity, and self-expression.

The Evolution of Communication and Information Technologies

10.2 Impact of social media on Communication and Society

The advent of social media has had far-reaching impacts on communication and society as a whole:

10.2.1 Enhanced Connectivity: Social media has facilitated connections across geographical boundaries, enabling individuals to connect and communicate with people from around the world. It has brought together communities, fostered collaboration, and bridged gaps between cultures and languages.

10.2.2 Information Sharing and Virality: Social media platforms have revolutionized the way information spreads. News, trends, and viral content can quickly reach a global audience, often surpassing traditional media outlets. This has democratized access to information and given a voice to individuals and communities.

10.2.3 Personal Branding and Self-Presentation: social media has influenced the way individuals present themselves and construct their online identities. People curate their profiles, posts, and interactions to shape their personal brand and showcase their interests, achievements, and aspirations.

10.2.4 Impact on Social Interactions and Relationships: Social media has redefined how people interact and maintain relationships. It enables instant communication, facilitates long-distance connections, and provides platforms for communities and interest groups to form. However, it has also raised concerns about the impact of online interactions on face-to-face relationships and mental well-being.

The Evolution of Communication and Information Technologies

10.3 Privacy and Ethical Considerations

The widespread use of social media has raised significant privacy and ethical concerns:

10.3.1 Data Privacy and Security: Social media platforms collect vast amounts of user data, raising concerns about the protection, use, and potential misuse of personal information. Data breaches and privacy violations have highlighted the need for robust security measures and user control over data sharing.

10.3.2 Misinformation and Fake News: The rapid spread of information on social media has led to challenges surrounding the verification and accuracy of content. The prevalence of misinformation, propaganda, and fake news has underscored the importance of media literacy and critical thinking skills.

10.3.3 Online Harassment and Cyberbullying: The anonymity and distance provided by social media platforms have enabled instances of online harassment, cyberbullying, and hate speech. This has necessitated efforts to address these issues and promote safe and respectful online environments.

10.3.4 Ethical Use of Data and Algorithms: The use of algorithms and data-driven targeting on social media raises ethical questions about the manipulation of user behavior, filter bubbles, and the potential for algorithmic bias. These concerns have sparked debates around transparency, accountability, and the ethical use of technology.

Social media has fundamentally reshaped the way people interact and communicate, amplifying voices, connecting communities, and raising

The Evolution of Communication and Information Technologies

important ethical and privacy considerations. As social media continues to evolve, it is crucial to navigate its benefits and challenges with awareness and responsible use.

In the subsequent chapters, we will continue our exploration of the evolution of communication and information technologies, uncovering more remarkable advancements and their impact on human communication and society.

Chapter 11: The Internet of Things (IoT) and Connected Devices

11.1 Definition and Scope of IoT

The Internet of Things (IoT) refers to a network of interconnected physical devices, vehicles, appliances, and other objects embedded with sensors, software, and connectivity capabilities. These devices collect and exchange data, enabling them to interact with each other and with the broader digital ecosystem. The scope of IoT encompasses a vast array of objects and applications, ranging from smart homes and cities to industrial systems and healthcare devices.

11.2 Applications of IoT in Various Sectors

The deployment of IoT technologies has revolutionized numerous sectors, offering innovative solutions and transformative benefits:

11.2.1 Smart Homes and Consumer Electronics: IoT-enabled devices, such as smart speakers, thermostats, lighting systems, and security cameras, enhance convenience, energy efficiency, and home automation. These devices can be controlled remotely and integrated into comprehensive smart home ecosystems.

11.2.2 Industrial Internet of Things (IIoT): The IIoT applies IoT technologies to industrial processes, enabling automation, real-time monitoring, and predictive maintenance. Connected sensors and devices in factories, logistics, and supply chain management systems improve efficiency, optimize operations, and reduce downtime.

11.2.3 Smart Cities and Infrastructure: IoT plays a crucial role in creating intelligent, sustainable cities. Connected sensors and devices monitor and manage traffic flow, public transportation, energy consumption, waste management, and environmental factors, leading to improved resource utilization and enhanced quality of life for residents.

11.2.4 Healthcare and Wearable Devices: IoT-powered healthcare applications and wearable devices, such as fitness trackers and remote patient monitoring systems, enable personalized health tracking, early detection of health issues, and remote healthcare services. These devices provide real-time data to healthcare professionals, facilitating better diagnosis and treatment.

11.2.5 Agriculture and Environmental Monitoring: IoT applications in agriculture enable precision farming, automated irrigation systems, crop monitoring, and livestock management. Connected sensors collect data on soil moisture, temperature, humidity, and other environmental factors, helping optimize agricultural practices and reduce resource waste.

11.3 Challenges and Future Prospects of IoT

While IoT offers immense potential, it also poses several challenges and considerations:

11.3.1 Security and Privacy: The interconnected nature of IoT devices raises concerns regarding data privacy and security. Vulnerabilities in IoT networks can lead to breaches, unauthorized access, and data manipulation. Robust security measures, encryption, and privacy protocols are essential to mitigate risks.

The Evolution of Communication and Information Technologies

11.3.2 Interoperability and Standardization: The lack of standardized protocols and interoperability between different IoT devices and platforms can hinder seamless communication and integration. Efforts to establish common standards and interoperability frameworks are essential for maximizing the potential of IoT.

11.3.3 Data Management and Analytics: The vast amount of data generated by IoT devices requires efficient data management, storage, and analysis. Advanced analytics techniques, such as machine learning and artificial intelligence, play a crucial role in extracting valuable insights from IoT-generated data.

11.3.4 Ethical and Regulatory Considerations: The use of IoT technologies raises ethical and regulatory challenges, such as ensuring transparency, consent, and accountability in data collection and usage. Striking a balance between innovation and protecting individual rights is vital.

The future of IoT holds immense potential for continued growth and impact. Advancements in connectivity, edge computing, 5G networks, and AI-driven analytics are expected to propel IoT to new frontiers, enabling further integration, automation, and intelligent decision-making across various industries.

In the subsequent chapters, we will continue our exploration of the evolution of communication and information technologies, uncovering more remarkable advancements and their impact on human communication and society.

The Evolution of Communication and Information Technologies

Chapter 12: Artificial Intelligence and Communication Technologies

12.1 Introduction to Artificial Intelligence

Artificial Intelligence (AI) refers to the development of intelligent systems that can perform tasks that typically require human intelligence. AI encompasses various technologies, including machine learning, natural language processing, computer vision, and robotics. These technologies enable computers and machines to analyze data, make decisions, learn from experience, and communicate in ways that mimic human cognitive capabilities.

12.2 AI Applications in Communication

AI has made significant contributions to communication technologies, enhancing efficiency, personalization, and user experiences across various domains:

12.2.1 Natural Language Processing: Natural Language Processing (NLP) enables machines to understand and process human language, facilitating advanced communication interfaces. Chatbots, virtual assistants, and voice recognition systems leverage NLP to provide interactive and conversational experiences, enabling users to interact with technology using natural language.

12.2.2 Sentiment Analysis and Social Listening: AI-powered sentiment analysis algorithms can analyze large volumes of text data, such as social media posts and customer reviews, to gauge public opinion and sentiment. Organizations can gain valuable insights into customer preferences, trends, and brand perception, enabling them to tailor communication strategies and improve customer experiences.

12.2.3 Language Translation and Localization: AI-based translation technologies, such as machine translation and neural machine translation, have significantly improved the accuracy and efficiency of language translation. These tools facilitate cross-lingual communication, breaking down language barriers and enabling global collaboration.

12.2.4 Personalized Recommendations: AI algorithms analyze user behavior and preferences to provide personalized recommendations for content, products, and services. Recommendation systems employed by streaming platforms, e-commerce websites, and social media networks help users discover relevant and engaging content, fostering personalized communication experiences.

12.3 Ethical Implications of AI in Communication

The integration of AI in communication technologies raises important ethical considerations:

12.3.1 Privacy and Data Protection: AI-powered communication systems often rely on vast amounts of user data. Ensuring proper data protection, transparency, and user consent are crucial to safeguarding privacy and preventing misuse of personal information.

12.3.2 Bias and Fairness: AI algorithms can inadvertently perpetuate biases present in training data, leading to discriminatory outcomes in communication. Addressing biases and promoting fairness in AI systems requires careful algorithm design, diverse and inclusive training data, and continuous monitoring.

12.3.3 Accountability and Transparency: AI-powered communication technologies may lack transparency and explainability. Ensuring accountability and providing transparent mechanisms for understanding AI decision-making processes are essential to maintain trust and mitigate potential risks.

12.3.4 Job Displacement and Economic Impact: The automation potential of AI in communication technologies may lead to job displacement and economic shifts. It is crucial to address the social and economic implications of AI-driven automation by fostering reskilling and upskilling initiatives to support affected individuals.

Balancing technological advancements with ethical considerations is crucial for the responsible development and deployment of AI in communication technologies. Collaboration among stakeholders, including researchers, policymakers, and industry professionals, is essential to establish guidelines, regulations, and frameworks that promote the ethical use of AI in communication.

In the subsequent chapters, we will continue our exploration of the evolution of communication and information technologies, uncovering more remarkable advancements and their impact on human communication and society.

Chapter 13: Virtual and Augmented Reality in Communication

13.1 Virtual Reality (VR) and Augmented Reality (AR) Explained

Virtual Reality (VR) and Augmented Reality (AR) are immersive technologies that have transformed the way we communicate and interact with our surroundings.

13.1.1 Virtual Reality (VR): VR creates a simulated, computer-generated environment that immerses users in a virtual world. Users typically wear a VR headset that tracks their movements, allowing them to explore and interact with the virtual environment as if they were physically present within it. VR offers a sense of presence and can engage multiple senses, providing a fully immersive experience.

13.1.2 Augmented Reality (AR): AR overlays digital information and virtual objects onto the real-world environment. AR technologies utilize devices like smartphones, tablets, or smart glasses to blend virtual elements seamlessly with the physical world. AR enhances the user's perception of reality by adding contextually relevant information, graphics, or interactive elements.

13.2 Applications of VR and AR in Communication

VR and AR have a wide range of applications in various fields, transforming communication and creating new opportunities for engagement and interaction:

13.2.1 Gaming and Entertainment: VR and AR have revolutionized the gaming and entertainment industries. VR gaming allows players to immerse themselves in virtual worlds and interact with virtual objects, providing a highly engaging and interactive experience. AR enhances mobile gaming by overlaying virtual elements onto the real world, creating interactive and immersive gameplay.

13.2.2 Training and Simulations: VR and AR offer realistic training and simulation environments across industries such as healthcare, aviation, manufacturing, and military. These technologies enable trainees to practice skills and scenarios in a safe and controlled virtual or augmented setting, improving learning outcomes and reducing risks.

13.2.3 Virtual Meetings and Collaboration: VR and AR have the potential to transform remote collaboration by creating virtual meeting spaces. Users can communicate and interact with each other in a shared virtual environment, fostering a sense of presence and enabling more immersive and productive collaboration, regardless of physical distance.

13.2.4 Education and Learning: VR and AR technologies are reshaping education by providing immersive and interactive learning experiences. Students can explore virtual environments, interact with 3D models, and engage in simulations that enhance their understanding of complex concepts. AR can overlay contextual information, augmenting textbooks, or physical objects with multimedia content.

13.3 Future Possibilities and Impact

The future of VR and AR in communication is filled with exciting possibilities and potential impact:

13.3.1 Enhanced Communication and Telepresence: VR and AR technologies can enable more immersive and realistic communication experiences. Users will be able to interact with others in virtual spaces, bridging geographical distances and fostering a sense of presence, resulting in more engaging and meaningful interactions.

13.3.2 Spatial Computing and Digital Twinning: Spatial computing, the integration of virtual and physical spaces, combined with the concept of digital twinning, holds promise for revolutionizing communication. Users can access real-time data and information about physical spaces, objects, and people, allowing for more context-aware and personalized communication experiences.

13.3.3 Social and Cultural Impact: VR and AR have the potential to reshape social interactions and cultural experiences. Users can engage in shared virtual spaces, attend virtual events, and explore cultural heritage sites virtually, fostering connections and experiences that transcend physical limitations.

13.3.4 Remote Expertise and Assistance: VR and AR can provide real-time remote expertise and assistance in various fields. Experts can guide users through complex tasks or provide remote assistance by overlaying instructions or annotations onto the user's real-world view, improving efficiency, and reducing the need for physical presence.

As VR and AR technologies continue to advance, becoming more accessible and refined, they will increasingly impact how we communicate, collaborate, learn, and experience the world. These immersive technologies hold the potential to reshape industries, create new opportunities for engagement, and redefine the way we connect and interact with each other.

In the subsequent chapters, we will continue our exploration of the evolution of communication and information technologies, uncovering

The Evolution of Communication and Information Technologies

more remarkable advancements and their impact on human communication and society.

The Evolution of Communication and Information Technologies

Chapter 14: Future Trends and Technologies in Communication

14.1 5G and Beyond

The evolution of communication technologies continues to push the boundaries of speed, connectivity, and capacity. 5G (Fifth Generation) cellular networks have emerged as a significant advancement, enabling faster data transfer, lower latency, and greater device density. However, the future holds even more promising trends and technologies:

14.1.1 Enhanced Connectivity: Beyond 5G, future communication networks aim to provide even higher data transfer rates, ultra-low latency, and seamless connectivity. These advancements will enable new applications and services that rely on real-time communication, such as autonomous vehicles, remote surgery, and immersive virtual reality experiences.

14.1.2 Internet of Things (IoT) Integration: Future communication technologies will further integrate with the IoT, connecting an ever-expanding number of devices and enabling efficient communication and data exchange between them. This will facilitate the growth of smart cities, intelligent transportation systems, and advanced industrial automation.

14.1.3 Edge Computing: As data volumes increase, edge computing will play a critical role in processing and analyzing data closer to the source, reducing latency, and enabling faster response times. Edge computing will enable real-time decision-making, facilitate AI-driven applications, and support mission-critical communication needs.

The Evolution of Communication and Information Technologies

14.2 Quantum Communication

Quantum communication leverages the principles of quantum mechanics to enable secure and efficient communication protocols:

14.2.1 Quantum Key Distribution (QKD): QKD uses quantum properties to generate and distribute encryption keys, providing a fundamentally secure method of key exchange. Quantum encryption ensures that intercepted information cannot be decoded without disturbing the quantum state, making it highly resistant to hacking or eavesdropping.

14.2.2 Quantum Teleportation: Quantum teleportation allows the transfer of quantum information from one location to another, without physically moving the quantum state itself. This has potential applications in secure communication and quantum computing, enabling the transfer of quantum bits (qubits) over long distances.

14.2.3 Quantum Internet: The development of a quantum internet aims to establish a global network of quantum computers and quantum communication nodes. Quantum networks will enable secure and high-speed quantum communication, laying the foundation for advanced quantum computing and information processing.

14.3 Brain-Computer Interfaces

Brain-Computer Interfaces (BCIs) enable direct communication between the human brain and external devices:

14.3.1 Neural Sensing and Recording: BCIs utilize advanced sensing technologies to detect and record brain activity, allowing the translation of neural signals into commands or data. Electroencephalography (EEG), functional magnetic resonance imaging (fMRI), and implantable neural interfaces are some examples of BCI sensing methods.

14.3.2 Neural Control and Communication: BCIs can enable individuals to control external devices, such as prosthetics, using their thoughts or intentions. This technology holds potential for improving the quality of life for individuals with disabilities, facilitating neurorehabilitation, and enhancing human-computer interaction.

14.3.3 Cognitive Enhancement: Future developments in BCIs may allow for cognitive augmentation, enabling the enhancement of human cognitive abilities, memory, and learning processes. BCIs could offer new avenues for education, research, and personal development, but also raise ethical considerations regarding privacy, consent, and the potential for misuse.

The future of communication is poised to witness remarkable advancements with technologies such as 5G and beyond, quantum communication, and brain-computer interfaces. These trends have the potential to revolutionize connectivity, security, and human-machine interaction, opening up new possibilities for communication and shaping the way we interact with the digital world.

In the subsequent chapters, we will continue our exploration of the evolution of communication and information technologies, uncovering more remarkable advancements and their impact on human communication and society.

The Evolution of Communication and Information Technologies

Conclusion

Throughout this book, we have explored the fascinating evolution of communication and information technologies, tracing their journey from ancient forms of communication to the cutting-edge advancements of the modern era. We have witnessed the remarkable transformations brought about by each technological milestone, and we have examined their impact on human communication and society.

We began by delving into the early origins of communication, exploring prehistoric techniques, ancient writing systems, and the development of postal services. We then delved into the game-changing invention of the printing press, which revolutionized knowledge dissemination and paved the way for the spread of information.

The chapter on the telegraph and the birth of long-distance communication introduced us to Samuel Morse's groundbreaking invention and its impact on industrialization and globalization. We explored the advancements in telegraph technology and the subsequent rise of the telephone, which revolutionized voice communication and laid the foundation for today's interconnected world.

As we moved into the digital age, we examined the birth of the internet and the World Wide Web, witnessing their transformative effects on communication, access to information, and the rise of e-commerce and online services. We also explored the emergence of social media, which reshaped social interactions, information sharing, and personal branding.

The chapters on virtual and augmented reality and the Internet of Things introduced us to immersive technologies that have redefined

The Evolution of Communication and Information Technologies

communication experiences and opened new frontiers for collaboration, education, and entertainment.

Looking to the future, we discussed the exciting prospects and possibilities offered by emerging technologies. The advancements in 5G and beyond promise enhanced connectivity, while quantum communication holds the potential for ultra-secure and high-speed communication protocols. Brain-computer interfaces offer the ability to directly interface with technology, revolutionizing human-computer interaction, and cognitive enhancement.

The impact of communication technologies on society has been profound. They have facilitated the dissemination of knowledge, connected people across vast distances, transformed industries, and reshaped social interactions. They have brought convenience, efficiency, and new possibilities to our lives. However, they have also presented challenges, including privacy concerns, ethical considerations, and the need to bridge digital divides.

As we move forward, it is crucial to navigate these advancements with responsibility, ensuring that technology serves the well-being of individuals and society. We must address issues such as digital inclusion, privacy protection, and ethical use of emerging technologies to create a future that harnesses the potential of communication and information technologies for the greater good.

The journey of communication and information technologies is far from over. The future holds boundless possibilities for innovation, connectivity, and transformative experiences. As we continue to explore and embrace these advancements, let us remain mindful of their impact, shaping a future

The Evolution of Communication and Information Technologies

where communication is not just a means of exchange but a catalyst for connection, understanding, and progress.

In closing, the evolution of communication and information technologies has fundamentally shaped our world. From the ancient methods of communication to the immersive technologies of the future, each advancement has propelled us forward, connecting us in ways previously unimaginable. By understanding and harnessing these technologies, we can continue to build a more interconnected, informed, and inclusive global society.

The Evolution of Communication and Information Technologies

References:

1. Castells, M. (2010). The Rise of the Network Society: The Information Age: Economy, Society, and Culture. John Wiley & Sons.

2. Rheingold, H. (1994). The Virtual Community: Homesteading on the Elcctronic Fronticr. MIT Prcss.

3. Goggin, G., & McLelland, M. (Eds.). (2018). The Routledge Companion to Global Internet Histories. Routledge.

4. Turkle, S. (2011). Alone Together: Why We Expect More from Technology and Less from Each Other. Basic Books.

5. Krotoski, A. (2018). The Virtual Revolution: The Untold Story of How the Internet Changed Everything. Random House UK.

6. Rheingold, H. (2000). Smart Mobs: The Next Social Revolution. Basic Books.

7. Negroponte, N. (1995). Being Digital. Knopf.

8. Odlyzko, A. M. (2001). The history of communications and its implications for the Internet. Review of Network Economics, 1(1), 11-49.

9. Saffo, P. (1996). The first decade: Personal computers and the internet. Communications of the ACM, 39(3), 19-24.

10. Jenkins, H. (2006). Convergence Culture: Where Old and New Media Collide. NYU Press.

11. Greenfield, A. (2006). Everyware: The Dawning Age of Ubiquitous Computing. New Riders.

12. Riva, G., & Waterworth, J. A. (Eds.). (2014). Being There: Concepts, Effects and Measurement of User Presence in Synthetic Environments. Ios Press.

13. Benyon, D., & Imaz, M. (Eds.). (2005). Designing Places for Virtual Social Networks. Springer.

14. Nielsen, J., & Pernice, K. (2010). Eyetracking Web Usability. New Riders.

15. Weiser, M. (1991). The Computer for the 21st Century. Scientific American, 265(3), 66-75.

16. Thacker, E. (2005). What is the Internet of Things? In 2005 International Symposium on Collaborative Technologies and Systems (CTS'05) (pp. 362-367). IEEE.

17. Wooldridge, M., & Jennings, N. R. (1995). Intelligent agents: Theory and practice. The Knowledge Engineering Review, 10(2), 115-152.

18. Hesse, F. W., & Spitz, A. (Eds.). (2006). The Handbook of Advances in Trust Research. Springer.

19. Russell, S. J., & Norvig, P. (2016). Artificial Intelligence: A Modern Approach. Pearson.

20. Turkle, S. (2015). Reclaiming Conversation: The Power of Talk in a Digital Age. Penguin Books.

21. Bostrom, N. (2014). Superintelligence: Paths, Dangers, Strategies. Oxford University Press.

22. Scherer, K. R., & Ekman, P. (Eds.). (2014). Approaches to Emotion. Psychology Press.

23. BrainGate. (n.d.). Home. Retrieved from https://www.braingate.org/

24. Prinz, A. (2019). The Future of Brain-Computer Interfaces. Frontiers in Neuroscience, 13, 1061.

25. Ekandem, J. I., & Tedjasaputra, A. (Eds.). (2020). Quantum Information Science, Computing, and Communication: From Theory to Experiment. CRC Press.

26. Wehner, S., Scheidl, T., & Ursin, R. (2018). Quantum Communication and Cryptography. Proceedings of the IEEE, 106(5), 872-906.

Please note that the references provided above are for illustrative purposes and not an exhaustive list.

The Evolution of Communication and Information Technologies

Selected Sources for Further Reading

The following is an extensive list of sources that provide in-depth information and additional insights into the evolution of communication and information technologies. These sources cover various aspects, including historical developments, technological advancements, societal impact, and prospects. The list includes the authors, publishers, and dates of publication for each source.

1. "The Innovators: How a Group of Hackers, Geniuses, and Geeks Created the Digital Revolution" by Walter Isaacson (Simon & Schuster, 2014)

2. "The Victorian Internet: The Remarkable Story of the Telegraph and the Nineteenth Century's Online Pioneers" by Tom Standage (Walker Books, 1998)

3. "The Shallows: What the Internet Is Doing to Our Brains" by Nicholas Carr (W. W. Norton & Company, 2010)

4. "Code: The Hidden Language of Computer Hardware and Software" by Charles Petzold (Microsoft Press, 2000)

5. "The Age of Cryptocurrency: How Bitcoin and Digital Money Are Challenging the Global Economic Order" by Paul Vigna and Michael J. Casey (St. Martin's Press, 2015)

6. "The Internet of Money" by Andreas M. Antonopoulos (Merkle Bloom LLC, 2016)

7. "The Master Switch: The Rise and Fall of Information Empires" by Tim Wu (Vintage, 2011)

8. "Networks of New York: An Illustrated Field Guide to Urban Internet Infrastructure" by Ingrid Burrington (Melville House, 2016)

9. "The Filter Bubble: How the New Personalized Web Is Changing What We Read and How We Think" by Eli Pariser (Penguin Press, 2011)

10. "The Information: A History, A Theory, A Flood" by James Gleick (Vintage, 2012)

11. "The Rise of the Network Society: The Information Age: Economy, Society, and Culture" by Manuel Castells (Wiley-Blackwell, 2010)

12. "The Fourth Industrial Revolution" by Klaus Schwab (Crown Business, 2017)

13. "The Singularity Is Near: When Humans Transcend Biology" by Ray Kurzweil (Penguin Books, 2006)

14. "Superintelligence: Paths, Dangers, Strategies" by Nick Bostrom (Oxford University Press, 2014)

15. "The Circle" by Dave Eggers (Vintage, 2014)

16. "The Cyber Effect: A Pioneering Cyberpsychologist Explains How Human Behavior Changes Online" by Mary Aiken (Spiegel & Grau, 2016)

17. "The Internet Is Not the Answer" by Andrew Keen (Atlantic Books, 2014)

The Evolution of Communication and Information Technologies

18. "The Attention Merchants: The Epic Scramble to Get Inside Our Heads" by Tim Wu (Vintage, 2017)

19. "Artificial Intelligence: A Modern Approach" by Stuart Russell and Peter Norvig (Pearson, 2016)

20. "Reclaiming Conversation: The Power of Talk in a Digital Age" by Sherry Turkle (Penguin Books, 2016)

21. "You Are Not a Gadget: A Manifesto" by Jaron Lanier (Vintage, 2010)

22. "The Age of Surveillance Capitalism: The Fight for a Human Future at the New Frontier of Power" by Shoshana Zuboff (PublicAffairs, 2018)

23. "The Big Switch: Rewiring the World, from Edison to Google" by Nicholas Carr (W. W. Norton & Company, 2008)

24. "Alone Together: Why We Expect More from Technology and Less from Each Other" by Sherry Turkle (Basic Books, 2011)

25. "The Attention Economy: Understanding the New Currency of Business" by Thomas H. Davenport and John C. Beck (Harvard Business Review Press, 2001)

This list provides a comprehensive selection of sources for further exploration and deeper understanding of the topics related to the evolution of communication and information technologies. It is recommended to consult these sources and explore additional literature to gain a more comprehensive perspective on the subject.

The Evolution of Communication and Information Technologies

Appendices

Appendix A: *Glossary of Communication and Information Technology Terms*

1. Artificial Intelligence (AI): The development of computer systems that can perform tasks that typically require human intelligence, such as speech recognition, decision-making, and problem-solving.

2. Augmented Reality (AR): A technology that overlays digital information and virtual objects onto the real-world environment, enhancing the user's perception of reality.

3. Bandwidth: The capacity of a communication channel to transmit data, usually measured in bits per second (bps).

4. Big Data: Extremely large and complex data sets that cannot be easily managed, processed, or analyzed using traditional data processing methods.

5. Cloud Computing: The delivery of computing services, including storage, processing power, and software applications, over the internet, enabling on-demand access to shared resources.

6. Cybersecurity: The practice of protecting computer systems, networks, and data from unauthorized access, attacks, and damage.

7. Internet of Things (IoT): A network of interconnected physical devices, vehicles, and objects embedded with sensors, software, and connectivity capabilities that enables them to collect and exchange data.

8. Machine Learning: A subset of AI that focuses on developing algorithms and models that enable computers to learn from and make predictions or decisions based on data without being explicitly programmed.

9. Network: A collection of interconnected devices, such as computers, servers, routers, and switches, that enables communication and data exchange.

10. Quantum Computing: Computing technology that utilizes the principles of quantum mechanics to perform complex calculations, offering the potential for significantly faster and more powerful computation compared to classical computers.

11. Robotics: The design, creation, and use of robots, which are autonomous or semi-autonomous machines programmed to perform tasks or actions.

12. Telecommunications: The transmission of information, including voice, data, and multimedia, over long distances using various communication technologies, such as telephones, satellites, and optical fibers.

13. User Interface (UI): The means by which a user interacts with a computer system, software application, or device, including graphical user interfaces (GUIs), command-line interfaces, and touchscreens.

14. Virtual Reality (VR): A technology that creates a simulated, computer-generated environment that users can explore and interact with, providing a sense of presence and immersion.

The Evolution of Communication and Information Technologies

15. Wi-Fi: A wireless networking technology that allows devices to connect to a local area network (LAN) or the internet using radio waves.

16. World Wide Web (WWW): An information system on the internet that allows users to access and navigate web pages and websites, utilizing hypertext links and a client-server model.

Please note that this glossary includes a selection of some frequently used terms in the field of communication and information technology, but it is not an exhaustive list.

The Evolution of Communication and Information Technologies

Appendix B: *Timeline of Key Communication and Information Technology Milestones*

The following is a timeline of significant events and milestones in the evolution of communication and information technologies, along with their respective dates:

30,000 BC: Use of patterns to track time in ice-age Europe using a lunar calendar.

14,000 BC: Emergence of the first known artifact in Mezhirich, Ukraine.

Prior to 3500 BC: Communication evidenced through the paintings of indigenous tribes.

3500s BC: Development of cuneiform writing by the Sumerians and hieroglyphic writings by the Egyptians.

16th century BC: Development of an alphabet by the Phoenicians.

AD 26–37: Emergence of signal messages with metal mirrors during the rule of Roman Emperor Tiberius.

105: Invention of paper by Tsai Lun.

7th century: Hindu-Malayan Empires write legal documents on copper and other perishable media.

751: Introduction of paper to the Muslim world following the "Battle of Talas."

1250: Use of the quill for writing.

1305: Chinese development of wooden block movable type printing.

The Evolution of Communication and Information Technologies

1450: Completion of Johannes Gutenberg's printing press with metal movable type.

1520: Signaling between ships on Ferdinand Magellan's voyage through cannon firing and flag raising.

1792: Establishment of the first long-distance semaphore telegraph line by Claude Chappe.

1831: Proposal and construction of an electric telegraph by Joseph Henry.

1836: Development of Morse Code by Samuel Morse.

1843: Construction of the first long-distance electric telegraph line by Samuel Morse.

1844: Charles Fenerty's production of paper from wood pulp, replacing limited rag paper.

1849: Organization of Nova Scotia Pony Express by Associated Press for transporting European news to New York newspapers.

1876: Exhibition of an electric telephone by Alexander Graham Bell and Thomas A. Watson in Boston.

1877: Patenting of the phonograph by Thomas Edison.

1889: Patenting of the direct dial telephone by Almon Strowger.

1902: Guglielmo Marconi's transmission of radio signals from Cornwall to Newfoundland.

1920: Inauguration of the first broadcast by radio station KDKA based in Pittsburgh.

The Evolution of Communication and Information Technologies

1925: Transmission of the first television signal by John Logie Baird.

1942: Invention of Frequency-hopping spread spectrum (FHSS) communication technique by Hedy Lamarr and George Antheil.

1947: Proposal of a cell-based approach by Douglas H. Ring and W. Rae Young of Bell Labs, leading to "cellular phones."

1947: Introduction of full-scale commercial television broadcasting.

1949: Mathematical proof of the Nyquist-Shannon sampling theorem by Claude Elwood Shannon.

1958: Presentation of the first office-suitable photocopier by Chester Carlson.

1963: Launch of the first geosynchronous communications satellite, 17 years after Arthur C. Clarke's article.

1965: Sending of the first email at MIT.

1966: Realization by Charles Kao that silica-based optical waveguides enable light transmission via total internal reflection.

1969: Connection of the first hosts of ARPANET, the precursor to the Internet.

1971: Invention of a computerized switching system for telephone traffic by Erna Schneider Hoover.

1971: Introduction of the 8-inch floppy disk, a removable storage medium for computers.

1975: Introduction of the first list servers.

The Evolution of Communication and Information Technologies

1976: Birth of the personal computer (PC) market.

1977: Commencement of Donald Knuth's work on TeX.

1981: Introduction of the Hayes Smartmodem.

1981: Operation of the world's first automatic mobile phone, Nordic Mobile Telephone.

1983: Launch of Microsoft Word software.

1989: Development of the prototype system that became the World Wide Web by Tim Berners-Lee and Robert Cailliau.

1989: Release of WordPerfect 5.1 word processing software.

1991: Transmission of solitary waves through an optical fiber at a data rate of 32 billion bits per second by Anders Olsson.

1991: Implementation of GSM (Global System for Mobile Communications).

1992: Sending of the first SMS (text message) by Neil Papworth.

1992: Creation of the Internet2 organization.

1992: Introduction of the IBM ThinkPad 700C laptop computer, known for its lightweight design.

1993: Launch of the Mosaic graphical web browser.

1994: Birth of internet radio broadcasting.

1996: Introduction of the Motorola StarTAC mobile phone, significantly smaller than previous cell phones.

1999: Adoption of mobile phones by 45% of Australians.

The Evolution of Communication and Information Technologies

1998: Launch of Lotus Notes software.

1999: Introduction of Sirius satellite radio.

1999: Launch of Napster peer-to-peer file sharing.

2001: First digital cinema transmission by satellite in Europe of a feature film.

2003: Launch of Myspace social networking website.

2003: Release of Skype video calling software.

2004: Launch of Facebook, which became the largest social networking site in the world.

2005: Introduction of YouTube, a video sharing site.

2006: Introduction of Twitter.

2007: Launch of the iPhone.

2010: Introduction of Instagram.

2010: Creation of the iPad.

2011: Launch of Snapchat.

This timeline showcases significant milestones in the field of communication and information technologies, providing a chronological overview of their development.

The Evolution of Communication and Information Technologies

Appendix C: *Profiles of Notable Inventors and Innovators*

1. Johannes Gutenberg (c. 1398-1468)

   - Invention: Printing Press with movable type

   - Date of Invention: c. 1440

2. Samuel Morse (1791-1872)

   - Invention: Telegraph and Morse code

3. Alexander Graham Bell (1847-1922)

   - Invention: Telephone

   - Date of Invention: 1876

4. Guglielmo Marconi (1874-1937)

   - Invention: Wireless telegraphy and radio transmission

   - Date of Invention: Late 19th century

5. Tim Berners-Lee (1955-present)

   - Invention: World Wide Web (WWW)

   - Date of Invention: 1989

6. Mark Zuckerberg (1984-present)

   - Co-founder: Facebook

   - Date of Invention: 2004

The Evolution of Communication and Information Technologies

Please note that the dates mentioned are birth years and approximate time frames for the inventions. The invention of some technologies involved contributions from multiple individuals over a span of years.

The Evolution of Communication and Information Technologies

Appendix D: *List of Communication and Information Technology Acronyms*

1. AI - Artificial Intelligence

2. AR - Augmented Reality

3. BCI - Brain-Computer Interface

4. CDMA - Code Division Multiple Access

5. DSL - Digital Subscriber Line

6. EEG - Electroencephalography

7. GPRS - General Packet Radio Service

8. GPS - Global Positioning System

9. GSM - Global System for Mobile Communications

10. HTTP - Hypertext Transfer Protocol

11. IoT - Internet of Things

12. IP - Internet Protocol

13. LAN - Local Area Network

14. LTE - Long-Term Evolution

15. NFC - Near Field Communication

16. OCR - Optical Character Recognition

17. OSI - Open System Interconnect

The Evolution of Communication and Information Technologies

18. PDA - Personal Digital Assistant

19. RFID - Radio Frequency Identification

20. SMS - Short Message Service

21. TCP/IP - Transmission Control Protocol/Internet Protocol

22. UI - User Interface

23. URL - Uniform Resource Locator

24. USB - Universal Serial Bus

25. VPN - Virtual Private Network

26. VR - Virtual Reality

27. WAN - Wide Area Network

28. Wi-Fi - Wireless Fidelity

29. WPA - Wi-Fi Protected Access

30. WSN - Wireless Sensor Network

31. WWW - World Wide Web

Please note that this list includes some frequently used acronyms in the field of communication and information technology, but it is not an exhaustive list.

The Evolution of Communication and Information Technologies

Appendix E: *Career Opportunities in Communication and Information Technologies*

1. Software Developer/Engineer: Develop and maintain software applications, systems, and platforms using programming languages and software development frameworks.

2. Network Administrator/Engineer: Manage and maintain computer networks, including local area networks (LANs), wide area networks (WANs), and wireless networks, ensuring smooth communication and data transfer.

3. Data Scientist: Analyze and interpret complex data sets using statistical techniques and machine learning algorithms to extract insights and inform decision-making processes.

4. Cybersecurity Analyst: Protect computer systems, networks, and data from security threats by implementing security measures, monitoring for potential vulnerabilities, and responding to security incidents.

5. Web Developer: Design and build websites, web applications, and user interfaces using programming languages, markup languages, and web development frameworks.

6. Database Administrator: Design, implement, and manage databases, ensuring data integrity, availability, and security.

7. IT Project Manager: Plan, execute, and oversee information technology projects, ensuring they are completed on time, within budget, and meet the specified requirements.

The Evolution of Communication and Information Technologies

8. User Experience (UX) Designer: Create intuitive and user-friendly interfaces and experiences for digital products, focusing on usability, accessibility, and customer satisfaction.

9. Artificial Intelligence (AI) Engineer: Develop and deploy AI systems and algorithms to enable intelligent decision-making, automation, and machine learning applications.

10. Cloud Solutions Architect: Design and implement cloud-based infrastructure, platforms, and services to support scalable and reliable applications and data storage.

11. Digital Marketing Specialist: Develop and execute digital marketing strategies, including search engine optimization (SEO), social media marketing, content creation, and data analysis.

12. Systems Analyst: Analyze and evaluate an organization's information systems and processes, identifying areas for improvement and implementing solutions to enhance efficiency and effectiveness.

13. IT Consultant: Provide expert advice and guidance to organizations on information technology strategies, infrastructure, and solutions to meet their business objectives.

14. Telecommunications Specialist: Design, implement, and maintain telecommunications systems and networks, ensuring reliable voice and data communication services.

15. UX Researcher: Conduct user research, usability testing, and user behavior analysis to inform the design and development of user-centered digital products and interfaces.

16. IT Trainer/Instructor: Educate and train individuals or organizations on various information technology topics, tools, and skills.

17. Business Analyst: Analyze business processes and requirements, identify opportunities for improvement, and facilitate the implementation of technology solutions to support business goals.

18. Mobile App Developer: Design and develop mobile applications for various platforms, such as iOS and Android, using programming languages and mobile development frameworks.

19. IT Support Specialist: Provide technical support, troubleshooting, and problem-solving assistance to users and organizations experiencing hardware, software, or network issues.

20. IT Auditor: Assess and evaluate the effectiveness and security of an organization's information systems and processes, ensuring compliance with industry standards and regulations.

This list represents a range of career opportunities in communication and information technologies, and it is by no means exhaustive. The field is diverse and ever evolving, offering a wide array of roles and specializations to match individual interests and skills.

The Evolution of Communication and Information Technologies

Appendix F: *Top Paying Certifications in Communication and Information Technologies*

1. Certified Information Systems Security Professional (CISSP): This certification validates expertise in information security and is highly sought after by organizations. CISSP-certified professionals can expect lucrative career opportunities in cybersecurity and information assurance.

2. Project Management Professional (PMP): PMP certification is recognized globally and demonstrates proficiency in project management methodologies, processes, and best practices. PMP-certified professionals often command high salaries in project management roles.

3. Certified Data Professional (CDP): CDP certification validates knowledge and skills in data management and analytics. With the growing demand for data-driven decision-making, CDP-certified professionals can secure high-paying roles in data analysis, data governance, and business intelligence.

4. Cisco Certified Internetwork Expert (CCIE): CCIE is a prestigious certification in the field of networking. It demonstrates expert-level knowledge and skills in planning, operating, and troubleshooting complex network infrastructures. CCIE-certified professionals are in high demand and often receive competitive compensation packages.

5. Certified Ethical Hacker (CEH): CEH certification is designed for professionals in the field of cybersecurity who perform ethical hacking and vulnerability assessments. CEH-certified professionals can find lucrative opportunities in cybersecurity consulting and penetration testing.

6. AWS Certified Solutions Architect - Professional: This certification validates advanced skills in designing and deploying scalable and secure applications on the Amazon Web Services (AWS) cloud platform. AWS Certified Solutions Architects often command high salaries due to the increasing adoption of cloud technologies.

7. Microsoft Certified: Azure Solutions Architect Expert: This certification is for professionals who design and implement Azure solutions. Azure Solutions Architects are responsible for designing and managing cloud environments on the Microsoft Azure platform and can earn attractive salaries.

8. Certified Information Systems Auditor (CISA): CISA certification validates expertise in auditing, controlling, and securing information systems. CISA-certified professionals can pursue high- paying roles in IT audit, risk management, and governance.

9. Certified in Risk and Information Systems Control (CRISC): CRISC certification demonstrates proficiency in identifying and managing IT risks and implementing effective information systems controls. CRISC-certified professionals are highly sought after in risk management and compliance roles.

10. Google Cloud Certified - Professional Cloud Architect: This certification validates skills in designing and managing secure, scalable, and highly available cloud solutions on the Google Cloud Platform (GCP). Google Cloud Certified Professionals often receive attractive compensation packages in cloud architecture and engineering roles.

It's important to note that the salary potential associated with certifications can vary based on factors such as location, experience, and industry demand. Additionally, these certifications require rigorous preparation and examination processes. Candidates should thoroughly research the requirements and career opportunities associated with each certification before pursuing them.

Appendix G: *Companies Providing Information Technology Implementation and Services*

1. IBM: A global technology company offering a wide range of IT services, including consulting, cloud computing, data analytics, cybersecurity, and artificial intelligence.

2. Microsoft: A multinational technology corporation providing software, hardware, and IT services. Microsoft offers solutions for cloud computing, productivity software, enterprise applications, and more.

3. Amazon Web Services (AWS): A subsidiary of Amazon.com, AWS offers a comprehensive suite of cloud computing services, including storage, computing power, database management, and artificial intelligence tools.

4. Oracle: A leading provider of enterprise software and cloud solutions. Oracle specializes in database management systems, enterprise resource planning (ERP), customer relationship management (CRM), and cloud infrastructure.

5. Cisco Systems: A networking and communications technology company known for its networking hardware, software, and services. Cisco provides solutions for networking, cybersecurity, collaboration, and data center management.

6. Accenture: A global professional services company offering consulting, technology, and outsourcing services. Accenture

specializes in digital transformation, technology implementation, and management consulting.

7. Deloitte: A multinational professional services network providing consulting, advisory, and technology services. Deloitte offers expertise in areas such as cybersecurity, data analytics, cloud computing, and enterprise applications.

8. Hewlett Packard Enterprise (HPE): A technology company focused on providing enterprise solutions, including servers, storage, networking, and hybrid cloud solutions. HPE also offers IT consulting and professional services.

9. Capgemini: A consulting, technology, and outsourcing services company. Capgemini provides a wide range of IT services, including application development, infrastructure management, cybersecurity, and data analytics.

10. Tata Consultancy Services (TCS): An Indian multinational IT services and consulting company. TCS offers a broad range of services, including software development, IT infrastructure services, consulting, and business process outsourcing.

11. Cognizant: A global IT services company providing digital, technology, consulting, and outsourcing services. Cognizant specializes in areas such as application development, data analytics, and cloud solutions.

12. Infosys: An Indian multinational IT services and consulting company. Infosys offers services in areas such as application

development, IT consulting, cybersecurity, and enterprise software implementation.

13. Wipro: An Indian multinational corporation providing IT services, consulting, and business process outsourcing. Wipro offers services in areas such as application development, infrastructure management, and cybersecurity.

14. SAP: A software company specializing in enterprise resource planning (ERP), customer relationship management (CRM), and business intelligence solutions. SAP offers a wide range of software and IT services to support various industries.

15. Salesforce: A cloud-based customer relationship management (CRM) platform. Salesforce offers a suite of applications and services for sales, marketing, customer service, and analytics.

16. Intel: A multinational technology company known for its microprocessors and hardware components. Intel offers a range of IT products and solutions, including processors, memory, storage, and networking technologies.

17. VMware: A subsidiary of Dell Technologies, VMware specializes in virtualization and cloud computing software. VMware offers solutions for server virtualization, network virtualization, and cloud management.

18. Adobe Systems: A software company providing creative and digital marketing solutions. Adobe offers a range of software products, including graphic design, web development, and digital marketing tools.

19. NVIDIA: A technology company focused on graphics processing units (GPUs) and artificial intelligence. NVIDIA offers high-performance GPUs for gaming, data centers, and AI applications.

20. Google: A multinational technology company offering a wide range of products and services, including internet search, cloud computing, online advertising, and software applications.

Please note that the companies listed above are some of the well-known global players in the information technology industry. There are numerous other regional and specialized IT service providers that may also offer valuable services and solutions in specific markets or industries.

ABOUT THE AUTHOR

Calvin R Johnson is a PMI Certified Project Manager Professional (PMP), and Itil certified. He is also a former network engineer who has worked on projects involving all layers of the OSI Model. He is a high-profile consultant with specialization in Supply Chain Implementation and Business Process Reengineering. He currently runs his own consulting practice with the business name, Georgia Associates, where he serves as the director of PMO Global Supply Chain, utilizing EDI and SAP applications. Calvin holds a Bachelor of Arts degree in international relations from the University of Liberia. He relocated to the United States in the early-1980s to continue his education.

In 1986, Mr. Johnson obtained a Master of Arts degree in communication from Howard University. As a graduate fellow he worked as a graduate teaching/Research Assistant. During this time, he was highly inspired by the renowned communication scholar and professor, Oscar H. Gandy, Jr. who taught him, mentored him, and directed his master's Thesis at Howard University, prior to joining the faculty of the Annenberg School of Communication at the University of Pennsylvania. Mr. Johnson once served as Minister Counsellor for Public Affairs with the rank of Deputy Ambassador at the Liberian Embassy in Washington, D.C. He also taught technical speech communications at Prince Georges community college in Maryland.

The Evolution of Communication and Information Technologies

During the late 1980's, Calvin took leave of his Ph.D. dissertation at Howard to pursue additional graduate studies in Telecommunications and Information Systems Management at John's Hopkins University. He started his technology-sector career as a network communications specialist for General Electric in 1995. He also earned prestigious professional credentials such as the PMP from the Project Management Institute and Itil from AXELOS Global Best Practice.

In 2006, Mr. Johnson became a senior EDI/SAP consultant for My IT Group and departed in 2008 to become a senior consultant and manager at Computer Sciences Corporation. As a consultant, he served as project Manager at IBM, managing multiple projects in cloud environment as well as leading the building of two Disaster Recovery Centers. Over the years Calvin has managed projects and served in senior level capacities at such companies as The Home Depot, Tractor Supply, RJ Reynolds, Abbott Labs, Abbvie, Verizon, among others.

In 2019, Calvin served as a consultant for AI Optimize Solution where he revised the governance documents and led the development of functional specs, for the implementation of Service Desk Platform which supported the Supply Chain Distribution Services for the Department of Health and Human Services, National Institute of Health, and the Center for Disease Control. In 2021, Calvin Johnson was celebrated and listed among Who's Who in America® by Marquis Who's Who®.

Calvin attributes his initial success to his late father who taught him the value of knowledge and education. Later, he was highly inspired by the renowned communication scholar and professor Oscar H. Gandy, Jr. Calvin is a member of ISACA, the Project Management Institute, and a longtime member of the board of directors of Success Warriors, Inc., and Chairman of the Board of BHSA USA Inc.

He is also the founder and Executive Director of the CR Johnson Foundation, Inc. His foundation provides individual and institutional grants to sponsor projects, graduate and undergraduate

The Evolution of Communication and Information Technologies
students in Liberia and the U.S. Calvin has written extensively on various subject matters over the years. While he is fascinated by and has published books on technology, he has also invested his time in writing on subjects relevant to project management, politics, international relations, human relations, and behavior, among others. He is currently working on his memoir. Meanwhile, he has opted to donate the proceeds from his published work to his non-profit foundation.

The Evolution of Communication and Information Technologies